LIZZARD LOOKS

Other poetry collections
by Prue Chamberlayne:

Beware the Truth That's Manacled (2022)
Locks Rust (2019)
*Ten Poets 2010:
University of East Anglia Anthology*

Prue Chamberlayne
LIZZARD LOOKS

2025

Published by Arc Publications,
Nanholme Mill, Shaw Wood Road,
Todmorden OL14 6DA, UK
www.arcpublications.co.uk

Copyright © Prue Chamberlayne, 2025
Copyright in the present edition © Arc Publications, 2025

The right of Prue Chamberlayne to be identified
as the author of this work has been asserted
by her in accordance with the Copyright,
Designs and Patents Act, 1988

978 1911469 96 4

Design by Tony Ward
Printed in the UK by
TJ Books, Padstow, Cornwall

Cover image:
'Gecko', 125 x 122 cm, mixed techniques on wood
© KRM (Chérif and Geza) - esprit du mur, 2023.

This book is in copyright. Subject to statutory exception and to provision of relevant collective licensing agreements, no reproduction of any part of this book may take place without the written permission of Arc Publications.

**Arc Publications UK & Ireland Series:
Series Editor: Tony Ward**

CONTENTS

SEASONED SCRIPT

Lifelines / 11
What we still seek / 12
Droplets on a Jolted Glass / 13
Cloven / 14
Flakes Keep Coming / 15
Fecundity / 16
So Quickly are First Hopes Reversed / 17
Severance / 18
Force in Frailty / 19
Seasoned Script / 20
Swivel of a Childhood Swing / 21
Fluorescence / 22
From a Bedroom Window in November / 23
The Afterlife of Vineyard Ledges / 24

ELEMENTAL

On Stepping Back / 27
Muse / 28
At Lake Level / 29
Cathedral-like / 30
From Minuscule / 31
Devil's Bridge, Ceredigion / 32
November at Zennor Head / 33
Off Smugglers' Lane at Chichester Harbour / 34
Morphosis / 35
'I must be in this place' / 36

WHAT THE ANGEL MIGHT HAVE SAID IN RESPONSE

Tenebrous / 39
Return of History / 40
Our Filaments Are Threadbare / 41
Pandemonium Manifesto / 42
She Speaks for Me! / 43
The Lure of Evil / 44
What the Angel Might Have Said in Response / 46

The Silver Coffee Filter on an English Mantelpiece / 48
An African Carving / 49
Wild Water / 50
Devouring Time, Blunt Thou the Lion's Paw / 51
Busselton / 52
Violets at Tourrettes-sur-Loup / 53
We Travel with Ghosts of Ourselves / 54
A Garden Door Reflects / 55
Windows / 56

AIR'S SO MUCH MORE THAN EMPTY SPACE

Summer Jet Black / 59
Murmuration / 60
Air's So Much More than Empty Space / 61
The Ruffetts / 62
Dunlins at Dawlish / 63
Weir / 64
Tin Pan Alley / 65
On Waking / 66
Layered Life / 67
Jeopardy / 68
For Facts or Artistry? / 69
Mutual Inquiry / 71
While Picking Tarragon / 72
Silent One / 73

Notes / 74
Acknowledgements / 76
Biographical Note / 77

SEASONED SCRIPT

LIFELINES

I have woven a parachute out of everything broken...
　　　　　　　　　　　　WILLIAM STAFFORD

Damage need not be a cause for lamentation –
consider the mending of ceramic vessels
with powdered gold and lacquer, Japanese confection
to a different preciousness, the breaks new channels,
oracular patterns, hieroglyphs that glint
on cups and bowls, kintsugi traced with fingertips.

WHAT WE STILL SEEK

In those cool places, hands announce themselves,
eloquent as faces of Madonnas – one holds
the child with fingers spread, the other points to bless –

huge in such carvings, they offer trust and hope,
as Gausbert, Austremoine, the local saints.
They speak from times when hands forged everything,

for me recall skin puffed with purple scratches
of those who cobbled shoes, pared hooves, laid hedges,
and after hours carved intricate designs.

Our woodman's hands are kitted up with gloves.
He leaves three root stumps by the door
that call to whittle to a new-found form –

hands more used to keyboard skills reach out
searching lines of growth within.

DROPLETS ON A JOLTED GLASS

Three perfect hemispheres,
each a bright eye,
the sunlit dark,

the shade side clear
with two black pupils
seeking mine.

A steadfast power,
meniscus holds them firm
within themselves,

to touch would break their grip,
whereas, untouched,
they can receive, transmit.

Does tension tire
on that sheer cliff?
Within earth's spin and tilt,

we humans too
must feel we're held
to keep our ground.

CLOVEN

Its chiffon skin defies the knife tip,
defends itself from human will
to render naked and then crush it
to add to vinaigrette or skillet.

A green wisp signals its intent –
shall I respect the life inside,
push into tilth to shoot and flourish
by snowdrops, daffodils and amaryllis,

first pause, to note the silky fondle
between my thumb and finger pad?
Shape of a tiny bagpipe sack,
flat sides, like a fritillary.

FLAKES KEEP COMING

Silence tautens
as if to whisper something wise

I want to keep this reach of feeling
crystals on face anoint bare skin

each splat of snow
lonesome as a vesper bell

gnarled trunks embalmed by the unearthly
emblems of claw-marks, some double back

glow of gold in forest glade
saffron schist turns indigo.

FECUNDITY

A single twig picked from the path
rings the vase with felted yellow –
how much from a whole copse, or forest?
Nectar for bees the news board says;
they've just emerged from winter burrows –
look out for upturned piles of sand.
Sunlight illumines drifts of dust
dense as galactic night-time skies
from probe of oak flowers. Nature labours –
imagine the hurdle of first seeding
when Earth was bare microbial mud.
Excess ensures against disaster –
    shoals of herring have re-amassed
    and wolves are spreading fast in France.

SO QUICKLY ARE FIRST HOPES REVERSED

Here, in winter's ragged tangle
tinge of lime turns chiffony,
far-reaching depths brought close
by crinkled leaves
that offer silk to sun;
oak pollen radiates gold.
Do I hear seepage
of the crystal liquid?

Slight shiver passes through
evoking veil of an eclipse,
hand hesitating on a child's curls –
more darkening
brings everything stock still
in dread, so quickly
are first hopes reversed.

Gilding returns, stays steady,
emerald shoots expand.
This pristine shine is brief as wetness
on a new-born calf
that soon will gambol,
clatter. Summer foliage
will stiffen, dappling transpose
to jet-black shade.

SEVERANCE

Bright, the tiny frills of fungi,
curls of cream and nutmeg puckered
as in Elizabethan ruffs –
they lure to touch as we discuss,

though we must keep our heads apart,
avoid close mingling of our breath –
this undue space a Hellespont
for sisters now long separated.

Footing slithers in the slime
but grabbing of an arm's forbidden –
trusted confidence awry,
inner warp and weft feel frayed.

FORCE IN FRAILTY

A pedestal of emerald
wraps the heel of a leaning hornbeam,
its braided bark in silver-green
fondled by strands from low-slung sun.

Rustle of feet through copper leaves
lightens the hush of winter lull.
Between the stream's bare labia
trickles a melody as it descends.

From pollards axed and lain as hedge
only connected by frailest strips
a forest of fine shoots has sprouted,
buds shut tight until unfurling.

SEASONED SCRIPT

Shafts from low-slung April sun
scribe black bars on bank and verge;

jagged across the lower terrace
they declaim as village elders

recalling the orchard drooped with lichen,
bulldozed flat from its two-way slope

where thistles, mint and dock would flourish,
new turf then churned by boars for roots.

These coal-black elongated stripes
nestle in emerald, darker in patches

from inner shade of longer grasses,
calligraphy only clean-cut

as long as buds of leaves and blossom
on uphill oaks stay tightly capped.

Sun-sidle of the script's sedate –
in contrast to pavane of birds

ornamented by a flit and trill –
and you might think the trunks exult

in double – as does my nib, probing
its way across this page, the shadow

urging its enjoyment, before
foreshortened by sun's higher rise.

SWIVEL OF A CHILD'S SWING

Dusk and dawn just fleetingly align
   when long-armed feathering
     scarcely daring to be there
       sweeps cornicing as passant
         only tethered in mind's eye

the gift of art to steady the gaze
   hold a point where the needle strikes
     claim from eternity out there
       the throb of energy that's ours.

         *

Woodblock of tendrils
   lattices and urban soot
     leaf skeleton
       soiled muslin or an angel's wing
        from slide and tilt of spin
        our hold on being

butterfly on stamen in a breeze,
   absence of stasis ecstasy.

FLUORESCENCE

The rough clump glints on sunny sill,
its clear cliff face, now pale quince jelly,
cast honey brown by passing cloud
until gold crags take shape again,
illuminated far inside,
conchoid, hexagonal, old spots and specks
from crystal world beneath our feet
where heat makes fault lines crack and split.

Gem energy transmits, receives,
as healer fingertips detect,
Sunrays traversing leaves outside
find echo in rock named fluoride.
Favrile light that's fluttering
through inner alchemy floats lines.

FROM A BEDROOM WINDOW IN NOVEMBER

I

At sunrise the mercurial birch
switches from lime to brandied copper;
little heart-shaped leaves amassed
    on purple strands

dangle from an arch-shaped branch
in silver white of forest steppe –
breast swell before an aria,
    here throne of doves.

II

Foliage flamed in saffron, aureate,
contorts in an orchestral frenzy,
Zangbeto's haystack shivering
    as evil is despatched;

each stitch figured in finery of kings
and tents of gold that shimmered far
at Guînes and Ardres – from this did Flöge
    dream Klimt's Kiss?

THE AFTERLIFE OF VINEYARD LEDGES

Mossed emerald skeins among tree trunks
form cabled ribs, each stone as stitch distinct.

Extent of this – on curves inclined
to full-day sun. Imagine the thud and clink,

still echoed in stonechats, blackcaps, local speech,
as rocks were levered, split, considered, dressed.

Taller walls retained the ancient tracks
where ox-carts carried stone so far, but how

to reach the in-between where dislodged boulders
thundered down at terrifying speed?

Many are trampled by cattle that roam
the woods for shade, their pathways guiding walkers,

hunters, mushroom pickers, myrtle seekers.
In Spring before new undergrowth, these walls stand out,

explain the big-beamed wine-press in the cave,
barrel hoops higher than a human head –

short-lived prosperity before phylloxera
caused exodus, an end to songs and repartee.

ELEMENTAL

ON STEPPING BACK

We rarely meet, but here wade in
    to silken glimmer of the lake,
follow the arc of rills ahead, ovals of silver
    that elongate, glide in and out of shape,
as green-black runnels ripple by.

An osprey unhurried floats into view,
    dives as a lance, soars up on languid wings.
We trace the architecture of our lives as laughter sparkles,
    furrow the stillness with our separate wakes,
return with offerings that astound, new skeins
    of thought to spur inquiry.

On sandy ledge we toy with lyrics in the making,
    an unfenced realm of letting happen
delicate as membrane under peeled-off pith.
    Mind flits to moonlight touch – best left unsaid –
or should forebodings be explored and faced?

MUSE

>Without you, here is odd, in woods
>with clack of clogs to deep-set mills,
>each granite slab a lain-on pillow.

So much we said, or left unsaid yet shared,
steps quickened with the spinning of suggestion
as thoughts in each like swallows winged and wheeled,

a spindle of spontaneous creation,
newness still blind to what we'd found
or what by each had been received or given –

a realm beyond the reaches of the mind
dance in nakedness of sleepwalk,
all armour shed, clear thought yet to arrive.

Then form found shape in the reverberation,
different things each knew donned new apparel –
like birdsong heard as reasoned conversation.

Rough-hewn towers gain decorated spires,
origins adopt new forms from interchange
with something unexplored, freshly acquired.

An artist often works alone all day,
but when musicians improvise together
some sensual entente comes into play,

and, yes, I longed to reach and touch bare skin –
voile curtains billow, hesitate, unfurl
and flap at how convention kicks –

>without you, here is odd, in woods
>with clack of clogs to deep-set mills,
>each granite slab a lain-on pillow.

AT LAKE LEVEL

Wet eyelashes gain sparkle-tips
as if florescent umbels

the stumble of a *cabbage white*
reveals solidity of air

and from the angle of a wavelet
gravity transmits a flash

silk-smooth ellipses slip from blue
to silver as I turn

each momentary miracle
an oracle, just mine

since no-one else is here
in this vast space…

I reach the diving rock where feldspar
hornblade, mica display

their pink and grey. A rill of silver
cobweb-thin loops round

in freefall of a passing soul
a tuft of thistledown drifts down

waves lap like wings, and turning back
towards the Stygian ravine

opacity, jet black, obliterates
all interplay of elements

portal to original dark matter.

CATHEDRAL-LIKE

Water at the weir's
steel lip
bronze flecked
from bracken
bridles at
the coming
endless tumble
edged by moss
on stones and trunks

    heart heaves
    at sunlit tawny plumage
    as a harrier lifts off

the track stays level
pipe cleaner birches
bend on slither slope –
through leafless tracery
a towering shaft of rock
thrusts up
against the wash of time,
old as starlight.

FROM MINUSCULE

Ashleworth, 2023

Moonlit behind etched blots of mistletoe
and cypresses around the cemetery,
a silvered serpentine with base-tone roar.

Glints in corners of the churchyard serve
as spirit level for seeped pools in aisles –
time to unscrew and ramp the pews.

Snowdrops stand bold by the buxom yew
where a wall-stile of jutted stones
offers infinity of sheen.

Under the metal gangway, deluge frolics,
impels to join the elemental swirl,
renunciate firm bank around the Quay.

There brimful river speeds to estuary and ocean,
roar where meadow-water dives back in,
gold gleam through brushwood on the other side.

All this from Welsh hill mist, massed flakes and raindrops,
swelled by tributaries along the way,
the minuscule accrued to the immense.

DEVIL'S BRIDGE, CEREDIGION

The water froths and whirls in sculpted circles
against the obstacle of rock, then glides
bog-brown before the next key leap.
Many have marvelled at the slender stone
that has withstood this force millennia long.

The lunge is through a vault that towers above.
Who could ignore the terror at such height?
Who'd dare to jump? It did not stop the ox,
but did deter the age-old owner
by whom the devil was outwitted –
bridge built in bargain for her soul.

Slippery steps descend to view what follows –
froth plunges into amber pools,
cascades pirouette from ledge to ledge.
The steepest drop supports a demon,
head bent back with jutting nose and chin,
in pensive mode amid ruched puckering.

From high-up encircled spinning, this pushing
through the narrow slit takes energy and risk,
and yet acceptance of constraint. Then feat
of freefall tumble into silvered flow.
Myth sprang from such a place. Aeons passed
for slime to separate as rock and water.
Gods and fauns portray the cruel and beauteous,
capture full-bloodedness we miss.

NOVEMBER AT ZENNOR HEAD

Clouds brood on moorland hills
though strands shred out towards the coast;

a southerly allays the incoming thrust
to billiard baize, brushed, groomed to smooth,

yet from the pivot point a boat tilts wildly,
flashes white; at jutting rocks

waves flounce vesuvial, a molten dance,
thunder thumps the caves beneath,

where St Senara's barrel landed with her infant,
and mermaid song lured Mathy Trewell.

The joust of wind turns sun to moon,
cloud in and out of being –

I too, a tattered rag in breeze,
transmute – is anything ever an entity?

OFF SMUGGLERS' LANE AT CHICHESTER HARBOUR

It's March, when tides creep high through fissures,
lap the furthest inlets between promontories
that stretch like fingers almost to the raging
entrance, twice-day turbulence at coming in
doubled in the cataract of sucking out;
it leaves a slime of green like finest hair
draped across a forest of black spikes.

Hard to stay upright on the velvet sludge
that leads to the embarkment spot
for summer ferries, this dark scene of stalks
and mud must then dry up – give way
to bogbean, blue flag, persicaria, and reeds –
a wild florescence that welcomed shadows
at night who knew degrees of moon, each track –
their footsteps laced sour smells with cognac.

MORPHOSIS

At Wittering a vast expanse of sand
bizarrely ribbed in places, elsewhere smooth
as if ironed flat. The glitter lies beyond,
where breakers in sporadic ranks suggest
a shallow sea with underwater banks.

Despite immeasurable shifts that drive it in
the lip of water edges forward, tentative,
waits at the cusp of time, weighs the tilting
of the Earth, desirous to delay
what's coming next, to guard the now, the frill
that brings new shine, the foam that will expire.
Will this organza slip beneath your feet,
render you weightless as Venus in the shell,
lift you as children skipping over waves,
their bodies moiréd in the haze of spray?

These thrusts are far too faint to engineer
the corrugations that will channel early dribbles
sideways. Corrugations form by heave
and haul of deeper water that shortly will invade
the full length of the shore, that pounding
already showing at the harbour neck
in sun-tossed crests of surf. A silvered veil
will slink along the unobtrusive slope
to fill the flatness with a dancing shimmer;
then rollick in triumphantly to offer greetings
to the brightly painted beach huts, the strips
of driftwood that yearn for dousing and adventure.

'I MUST BE IN THIS PLACE'

You'll come? Gun-metal grey
shoots spray – delivers seaweed wads
threaded with green reeds –
    what is at play?

Bare skin on grass and grit
to ginger sand – foamed waves knock
thighs and face – don't think –
    plunge in – to lift –

the first translucent crest
cross-cut by next – and next – spit brine –
too fast to breathe in time –
    lungs seared in chest –

piteously – legs flail
to gain the milder ruck behind –
watch orange orb descend
    to layer of grey –

the patch of brimstone glint
eludes, falls short – cringe cold dictates
we turn from hope to fight
    the swell by will

gainsay lithe undercurrent –
avoid plumed thwack at groynes – emerge
in streaming sand to lurch –
    sting and delight.

Indoors his canvasses
of barnacles and rocks – all this you've shared –
the finch that came each day –
    and something steadies.

WHAT THE ANGEL MIGHT HAVE SAID IN RESPONSE

TENEBROUS

All of us, among the ruins, are preparing for a renaissance beyond the limits of nihilism. But few of us know it.
　　　　　　　　　　　　CAMUS, *The Rebel*

Are dreams being hammered into coffins?
We know our apple's rotting at the core
inside its flaunted lustrous skin.
I'm not abandoning my mother tongue.

RETURN OF HISTORY

> *William Ellis aged 12, son of Qualquey Assedew from Guinea, baptised in Stroud in 1801.*

Through tumbling hills and gardens our train draws in.
The station might be Adelstrop – but here
girls cluster, the uniform maroon,
straight necks with Afro coifs, their talk intent,
and my heart bounds – before revolt at what comes back
online – *Most students of white heritage.*
These girls would shake that school – *I love being black* –
fuel the truth that brings new shame at mansions
from slave-based wealth, broadcloth for redcoats,
trade worldwide that draped these slopes
in crimson, blue, for Oriental rule.
Pride lights in those who rose as activists,
    bolts break, long silence yields and ricochets
    a different reckoning, within these hills.

OUR FILAMENTS ARE THREADBARE

Cherry Wood, Nov 2023

Dark spots on path, yet coffee tempts. Beneath the canvas
infants stay intent on play. A bright-eyed toddler
wanders freely, steadied by his father's gaze.
Dog noses its ball close to my toe.

At corded deluge, chairs screech tighter. *Thunder,* predicts
a weathered face – loud as a bomb right overhead.
Dog knew first, he tells a woman, whose eyes recall
Fayum sarcophagi. As war-time boy

he'd seen a fire-ball twist and burn a barn with cattle,
rob them of buttermilk. *That's good for scurvy,*
says portrait eyes, bare limbs against the tanks in mind –
More spilt blood than drinking water,

where hell-fire rockets trace night sky, and targets flare,
yet still teens dance, hold hands, stamp feet, shoulders aligned,
stretchers tilt and speed, newborns packed tight for warmth,
Throb of breath on shores of death.

What happens to our souls, we who sip drink and fret
at having left the heating on? A small child forced
into its pushchair howls and thrashes in despair.
Weep for the lives your wishes never led.

PANDEMONIUM MANIFESTO
– after Georg Baselitz

What thoughts had ricocheted round that living room
as men donned uniforms, the port was bombed,

camps nearby for Roma, gays. What whispers
lingered in the head-high currant bushes?

Among the trumpeters did I sense discord,
a halting measure in the Spring parade?

Why such fervour over grace at meals?
Why such cherishing of an English girl?

Frau Klemer brushed the photo of her son,
blonde and white-uniformed, with her thumb;

Herr Lange grimaced at the plunder of a ship,
his men grabbed flour, their bellies split –

no word of yellow stars, of ash,
firestorms depositing blobs of melted fat.

Tongues loosened with the fallen Wall – a grandmother
recounting waltzes with Nazi officers.

Baselitz recast my memories,
linked them with vermin, worms on walls.

SHE SPEAKS FOR ME!

In tribute to Christa Wolf's City of Angels

As dreams from Spring-time politics at home caved in,
you, outspoken oppositionist who'd risked your skin,
faced media slaughter as a leftist heroine.

I shared your love for your fast disappearing home,
not for its pampered bureaucrats and thought control,
but for the equal sharing of the world, the hope

and goals the best had fought for over centuries
at cost of lives and liberty, the fundaments achieved,
defended, and now being handed to barbaric greed.

I know the loneliness you felt in the US
where no one understood the nature of your loss –
What I've never lived I know I'll always miss.

You share your agonies in peeling through the past,
your loss of mind in levering memories to surface,
We cannot live without forgetting offered solace.

You kept your pride and principles. In such dark times
did I renege? Well yes. Kept quiet, used euphemisms
like *militant* and *activist* – turned to realms

of inner life, thought hopes of vibrant communism
sunk, and so lapsed in complacency.
Your self-interrogation stirred me deeply –

and history turns! Now poisoned seas and mass disease
force future-looking. Children challenge, *How have you lived?*

THE LURE OF EVIL

As octopus my reach can cripple you
    and wring your breath, yet I look innocent
until I strike – surprise a devious tool –

weird colours of my suckers beckon and tempt,
    as does my finery slick typhoons,
my showy claim to be benevolent.

I am defined by all the harm I lead to,
    from Nagasaki and Iraq, to ruining
a child's well-being by abuse.

It puzzles how early cruelty began
    given the Paradise provided – why flay,
cut tongues and ears, devour a person's brain?

Torture of slaves and heretics gave way
    to 'terrorists' – who more offends,
the lyncher or the throngs that jubilate?

I work in the far depths of people's minds,
    for children I'm in wardrobes, pavement cracks,
boy's memory of belting in a garden shed.

Folktales toughen innocents against worst fears –
    do some pervert, and predispose to sadism,
as when a 'witch' is pitched into the flames?

There's so much scope in family terrain,
    old feuds, bitterness, and sexual appetite –
rapists shut their minds to life-long stain.

I now train secret agents to insinuate
    themselves in private lives, bear kids in stealth,
to gather information for the state.

Heroes who strive for change are vilified,
  eliminated. Unending wheel,
rendering modest Tamerlane's tower of heads.

I'm everywhere, as slippery as an eel,
  from party games to planetary schemes.
Yet my opponent, life force, might win still –

grotesquery in Day of Judgement scenes
  performs with energy, the blessed look bland,
but novel schemes burst out, we're neck-a-neck.

Frankly, I'm glad – I need to be reined in.

WHAT THE ANGEL MIGHT HAVE SAID IN RESPONSE

Leuven University Tower, January 2020

At the entrance to the tower,
an Angel, as if she's just alighted
with a thought that took her by surprise.

Rough brown wood
enfolds her in ribbed
curlicues of fabric, wings and hair,
her eyebrows, fingertips and lips alert.
Is she in discourse with her soul?
One should not interfere.

I long to share that sense
of being anchored to the core,
and she stays unperturbed when I step near.

*

The fragile iron staircase
coils up to five more floors –
the rail as crutch,
eyes on next step.
Shock photos at each level –
Old Market Square
with mangelwurzels, artichokes,
crockery and broiling pots
laid out on the ground –
reduced to rubble;
this tower in cinders;
boots and swagger
of someone's father, lover,
perhaps your cousin.

The bells are huge –
what horrifying dissonance
when they crashed down
from that great height,
the carillons so delicately tuned.

*

High in vertiginous wind,
church spires toy-size,
images assail – howl of a child
prised from a concrete wedge
and seas of ragged tents.

What would the Angel have said then?
And what would she say now?

At the descent she's there,
intent. O for a quick embrace –
vigour of limbs
mutually attuned,
hope frail, and yet preeminent –
before the cold stone stair.

THE SILVER COFFEE FILTER ON AN ENGLISH MANTELPIECE

The bandings look like peasant leggings
of Silesian diggers long ago
who followed lustrous specks in veins
down shafts and slippery galleries.
The shade side's rich in tarnished orange,
while light side sparkles –
how often was it burnished
in those vivacious places filled
with wit and music, coffee vapour?

At such a table, white cloth starched,
its saucer ring astride a cup,
two knobs ensured no finger smudge.
The strength of flavour was adjusted
by a screw inside – too hot to hold,
perhaps the waiter's gloves obliged.
Once coffee drained, the lid,
so pretty with its petal handle,
served as saucer against drips.
Not from Vienna, says a connoisseur –
art deco, debelloire from Paris.

If mankind perished, could that same path
from specks to artistry ever be traced again?

AN AFRICAN CARVING

Two men sit on the mantelpiece – they look ahead,
so still that they arrest my gaze each day
and might be praying. Elbows on knees and rim
steady the canoe, chins tether knuckles.

Dugouts abound worldwide since ancient times,
trees cut with fire and adze, trunks burnt and scraped
to shape and render hollow. The sturdiness
recalls a raft for cars that pulled and swayed
on chains across a wide-swept river – and saplings
straddling a ravine, like driving on a hammock.

With chink of grit and clunk of clod, Adam
delved aeons earlier than speech, for tilth
that *all to sweetness turns*. Village women
hoed sugar beet and flirted with my father,
laughter syncopated with deft twists.

To dig for gold, men dared high seas, risked treachery
and theft in threadbare camps to seek new lives.
The driver of an opencast machine,
who whirls up clouds of topsoil and microbes,
flicks digits, his mind consoled by Eve's pop songs –
their boss, Ball's gentleman, an oligarch.

Whereas Assange, who dug in files to ferret out
what we, for life, most need to know, is lashed.

WILD WATER

    Zambia 1967

In scorching heat of orange earth
and zinging insects I take two visitors
on walkabout beyond our school
through spindly *cassia* scrub,
mopane trees. Then miracle –

a stream cascading down in runnels
through rocks and glinted spin of pools
too small for hidden crocodiles –
water safe in such a torrent
from parasitic *mubongola*.

Toes on smooth stone, my two companions
lift shifts heavenwards, tall bodies
pre-Raphaelite in silken whiteness,
one hazel-tufted, the other blonde.
I'm stunned by their audacity,

long for rippled cool on my skin,
but people could pass silent in the dust –
I'm caught in fears of cultural affront,
shy to show my body lines,
my 'freedom' now exposed as shallow.

I'm here to learn beliefs and customs –
do women bare thighs or pussy parts?
Do others stare? Were swimmers nude
at Gilf Khebir? Strange, too, no sense
of water's sacredness –

when the fish-tailed snake, *Nakamwale*,
draws human shadows into lakes,
the person dies; blemished babies
are discarded in such places.

What were we, by stepping into,
desecrating, trampling on?

DEVOURING TIME, BLUNT THOU THE LION'S PAWS

Yallingup, Western Australia

I breathe the early morning air,
and scan the distant line of sea
where billowed sails swept in,
watch parrots sidle on a phone wire,
crimson, emerald and citric
stitched against the sky.

Then only yards away,
a six-foot kangaroo
with bulbous eyes, scarred jowls,
a jutted muzzle, earlaps erect.
Stock still, he stares at me,
is fear or intimacy the danger?

Could brinkmanship lead to
new transport? Shall I
edge nearer? Is he too
in a riptide? Just us, no being
of either kind need know.

Sense calls for nonchalance,
resumption of my parrot-gazing.
Glance back, and off he's bound,
sway of his bulk, thick tail
like netted cargo on a wharf.
Order and emptiness return.

At night, for full-strength stars
away from lights, I follow stones
that edge the track, wish one more step
to press full length against his pelt.
He'd lay curved claws upon my shoulder,
transport me to primordial times
before the ships and guns,
when paths, rocks, trees and sacred sites
were voices held in veneration.

BUSSELTON

Those boys on bikes
wild copper hair, long limbed,
with soft round faces defy
state laws and calculations.
Ancestors are in mass graves –
their leaders know the places.

VIOLETS AT TOURRETTES-SUR-LOUP

> Étranger, je sens bon. Cueille-moi sans remords:
> les violettes sont le sourire des morts.
> Paul-Jean Toulet

A flirty scent that comes and goes,
a girl's desire that chances all –
a flower that sprang from Adam's tears.

Bestowal of perfume to the leaves
won Vulcan his first kiss from Venus;
bestirred for Sappho lost lesbian love;

in Egypt violet eyes denoted
spirit people in communion
with the musk of life beyond.

Napoleon chose for his return
the season suffused with their faint odour.
Why else would night-time trains to Paris

transport bouquets for sale at stations,
perfume for syrup, soap and lotions
and crystallised *confiserie*?

High on the cliffs of this *bastide*,
houses tower – wealth accrued
from vertical columns and tight-packed rows.

Modesty shrinks, and yet can hold
its place in history from chink of wall…

WE TRAVEL WITH GHOSTS OF OURSELVES

Ranked seatbacks under slats of light splay out
across embankments streaked by speed;
winter wheat gains succulence on slowing,
thinned poplars meld autumnal colours;
smudged grey, my own face palely reaches heaven.

Deep in the hedge a woman yawns –
by mirror moves I can erase the smears
that compromise her features. A man
who hasn't slept for weeks, slack mouth, ashen skin,
sways up the aisle, more pallid still in vegetation.

On Orwell's mudflats treetops foxtrot,
pylons tango, plying kite strings,
cat's cradle strands, inside pulled out –
our fantasies less idle than they seem,
antechamber to the world of dreams.

A GARDEN DOOR REFLECTS

When closed, my several panes look out
at nut trees, washing line, deer nibbling
flowers of my surrounding vine,
snakes suspended from the gutter
furling wildly while they couple.

Doors open, I see myself reflected
in my twin – the spattered grass-cuts
doubled, brushed off occasionally
by this same person sitting here
enjoying shade from scorching sun –
she caught the image I threw back
and took this photo, which she likes.

It may take time to puzzle out
she's not behind me, but in front.
Since I face north the only brightness
is borrowed from my opposite.
Her portrait's barred by frames of panes
as if she's brandishing a cross –
the kind cemented into stone
just up the track and wrapped in brambles.

Shade-side brings ghouls from the rough stone wall,
massive cheeks and deep-set eyes.
But in the sunlight she's self-possessed,
with mellow air and glowing skin,
her forearm witness to farm beginnings –
buckets of pig swill poured into troughs,
sacks and straw bales humped about –

she'd feel less sure on a dance floor,
until scenes changed to rock and swing.

WINDOWS

She loves those on the valley side,
their heights and angles to the view.
Westward, at dawn, they frame magenta,
departure of the full-round moon,
each evening a different sunset blaze.

And they receive – bell's Angelus,
kulning for cows at milking-time,
bats' hover, their flit-in to dangle,
splatter pee and turds all night,
footsteps in desiccated scrub –
hare, boar, deer, shade of a lover.

Absence brings tarnished mirrors,
bird shit dribble, drooped cobweb lace;
lizards startle out of grooves;
graveyards of peacocks, admirals,
speckled gauze wings, upturned scarabs –
nature's artistry in each.

The furthermost may offer glimpses
of squirrels rippling on lateral branches.
There where honeysuckle exudes
nightlong, float wavering laments
and shrieks of owls, metal gutters'
taps and clinks, thunder's drum-roll.

Ordered moonbeams shift through rooms,
enact this in-out dialogue.
At times she feels a ghost between the ancient
and her passing, and yet the plenitude of nature,
the fling and venturing of senses,
roots her presence in this place.

AIR'S SO MUCH MORE THAN EMPTY SPACE

SUMMER JET BLACK

The walk begins in feathered light
of ash and elder. Quiet voices
in a garden's darkest spot
sustain the cool, while all too soon
sand glares on sun-baked track.

The woodland shade ahead is dark
as underworld of caves where bison
ripple in a passing flare.
At once in that black mass,
each nettle, insect shines distinct,
beech leaves lit as green-gold specks
dance on the silver sleek of trunks.

No glint, no matt in the solidity
of summer black – flat shadow of an oak
transfixes in a new-mown field.
So Soulages panels in *outre-noir*
still all agitated thought,
draw to another sphere of being.

MURMURATION

Shape-shifting dark that stays yet sways,
almost dissolves to faintest grey,
speech bubble above a winter wood –

how long does it take to realise
the change as tilt, wings flipping
to linearity, sublimely timed?

I yearn to be propelled among them,
to know how they avoid collision
in morphic resonance too fast for thought.

They switch and fold like fish –
some principle of magnetism
keeps the pace and undulates.

Northern lights shift fan-like,
clouds sail in dark but pass –
no somersaults in choreograph.

It seems the very form's alive,
more than haphazard in its beauty –
perhaps they shape a giant bird

to terrorise their predators
before the roost in nearby woods –
fluttered restlessness unearthly.

AIR'S SO MUCH MORE THAN EMPTY SPACE

Hell is empty and all the devils are here.
                                    THE TEMPEST

Our ancestors had Gods
who strode from ochre clouds they used
as chariots and thrones; cherubs
forced wind from bulbous cheeks –
    sky was Gods' thoroughfare for Greeks.

In summer, volcanic cumuli
gold with an underlay of ash
shimmy in contrary directions –
low down, a drape of grey descends,
    darkening from East to West,

shrouding syncopates in drips.
As sunlit rods of glass advance
a quarry tumbles rocks on planks,
calico rips the firmament,
    sockets inside sizzle and snap,

translucent beads lance levelly,
melt instantly. Rain on tarmac
cups in military ranks,
trees heave and thrash, while orange blaze
    conveys the scale of power unleashed.

Cocoons of mist, until, lime-green,
a mound floats up, monk's pate ringed
in woodland tonsure. The sun conducts,
bids mountains to pyramid, to shrink –
    soon they glower in seaweed green.

A small medallion of silver
glints, its quiver stilled. How did it
reach a floor indoors, intact?
Kneel, in homage to this gem,
    its journeying.

THE RUFFETTS

The valley's laid out wide before her,
flood plain of cinnamon and green
with glimpses of the winding river;
below, the steep-banked lane soon ends
in apple orchards, sheds and meadows.

The hillside where she's propped on tussocks
tufted between brambles, briars,
rustles with melody and scurry
of creatures free, not tied or fenced.

Here, away from farmhouse chores,
mother's aches on flagstone floors,
small inner flames flare into light,
linger like butterflies in her mind
long enough to be believed in –
such moments beckon as true living.

She loves the quiet of panther power
in Rilke, his lilt of language on terrors
of our secret being – such heights
unreachable as cumuli
that tower above majestically.

DUNLINS AT DAWLISH

What seems at first a horde of voles
turns Lilliputian ballerinas,
glissade of black leotards
circling pebbles, seaweed strings
before the encroaching skirt of sea.

In twist, like thoughts too quick to catch,
white undersides switch striped then black –
oh, to match their acrobatics,
dissolve, cast soul to salt-flecked wind.

But they drop back to peck dry sand,
fly in a flurry to the loop of ebb;
ruffled speckles double in the sheen,
barre-trained dancers heads erect,
legs held taut against the swill.

WEIR

At the bend
the water's racing with itself
bubbles gleeful at the speed

how is this seamlessness sustained
as never a gap in air to breathe

effect of pressure
a physicist explains –
but there's a gap between our minds.

TIN PAN ALLEY

Rain concocts patterns, fluted
on a tarmac lane, herringboned in swill,
then pebbled, as a peacock's tail.

Three wide roofs of graded lauzes
act as washboards and maracas,
claves of rainfall syncopate the rhythm,

rivulets along the length sway in,
metallic gutter-music surges,
gulps and spouts to the next level.

Is body music tuned, attuned,
in time with outside sounds – nature's
measure in our minds and dreams?

ON WAKING

My fuddled mind at slate grey dawn
gnaws at stealth of urban thrum,
same unease in woodland trees
when pelt of rain on sludge of leaves
pads up close like felted feet,
and roar of train or motorway
resolves as conifer wind-seethe.

Downstairs on grit a footstep jolts,
gravelled greetings between mates,
laughter and joking in Balkan tongue
surface from the indistinct –
quickened beat of a jazz band.

LAYERED LIFE

Below the pomegranate lights
that stud the night from cranes and towers
sewers choke with balls of fat,
effluvia of body juice;

a hell-hole screech near Camden Town
tunnels through the marsh substratum,
cables, pipes in soot-black loops
arteries of our existence.

Rats are discrete – one sauntered through
the bedsit once, just sniffed and left –
dangling blankets hoisted up,
prayers bed legs too sheer for claws.

At Charing Cross where trains still trundle,
the river wallops Whistler pillars,
Stygian dark with glints of scarlet
slaps its gimmickry at Shard and Gherkin.

JEOPARDY

And there the skeleton of a deer
laid flat, plain bone, but all intact,
one hoof still furred, as if it might
spring into a new form of being.

Thoughts swarm like carrion flies – a wolf
would tear the corpse, as would a raptor –
an army of flesh-eating beetles?

In dream a clump of leathered skin,
departed life on bare dry ground,
animal hide or someone's coat.

That headless doe with blown-up belly
close by our home haunts still. A trophy?
A neighbour buried her, but I check the mound.
    Substantial, somehow not quite dead.
    Substantial, somehow, not quite dead.

FOR FACTS OR ARTISTRY?

One step in the secadou
squeak at my heel, a bat
with gauze-like wings stretched on the lintel;

thread-like claws
scrabble at empty air,
the mole-furred body still – as if concussed –

rare chance
to see those rose-bud lips
pucker in a pitiful mewl. I try to reach

the soot-black slats,
but it flips back to dangle
one-clawed from the rough wood door.

Then murmurings
from another shed –
a drama sensed, was this one telling?

A search presents
a cram of facts on diet,
physiology and flying habits,

myriad insects
vacuumed, minced, compressed
in jet-black pellets, splatches of yellow pee.

Metrics astound,
but would I not prefer
to hang from a rafter in ruminative mood,

pause to wonder
at translucent wings
veined like petals of a cuckoo flower?

The several joints
switch for deft flight, as fine-tuned
sails are angled, these for swift careening

in midge-filled air,
antennae modify
at lightning speed, far faster than a blink,

height of flight
three thousand metres – but no comparison
with air scud past my hair.

MUTUAL INQUIRY

A glide of silk
along my heel

at edge of step
stops breath –

a lizard, head
looped back, transfixed –

        at sandal –
        not part of ledge!

Sun-spot illumines
the emerald belly,

it pecks at moss,
throat working hard,

        tiny tesserae
        black-threaded,

then stands up, statuesque,
eyes turned to me –

dwelling still
on the encounter?

        As I step forward
        it disappears –

but no, it's there,
alert – tempted

to another contact?
Surprise our engine of inquiry.

WHILE PICKING TARRAGON

That mass of chequered black-yellow-white
unravelling might lash in panic –

my feet decide, leap off the ground
towards seclusion of the house,

gut riotous – beauty and terror
mordantly entwined.

No trace of escape through marigolds
and mint, past compost box – finesse

in that stout weight – but why repose
at that frequented spot? Just drunk

from canicule, or gorged on slugs,
relief at hatching out of eggs –

catch of heart each time on finding
yet another lace-like skin.

SILENT ONE

At evening with no shriek or jabber, the jay
glides in, perches on a low-down twig
remaining from a severed stump, sails
to a stone in fine-ground soil, where swing and clink
of *l'élagueur* sheared branches, pitched whine and thump,
from which had sprung in wobbled flight four fledglings.

She's surely checking – cocks her head and peers
at that spot, her home, then us, requesting
restitution. A fortnight long this honouring
continues, lament for lives, appeal for recognition
of collateral in opening space for skies.

NOTES

'Seasoned Script' (p. 20):
   The Pavane is a stately 16th / 17th French dance in slow duple time, usually performed in elaborate clothing.

'Our Filaments are Threadbare' (p. 41):
   Written on Nov 30, 2023, Day 22 of the Gaza bombing;
   The final lines of stanzas 4 and 5 respectively are from W.H. Auden's 'Anthem for St Cecilia's Day', 1940.

'Pandemonium Manifesto' (p. 42):
   Painting (1962), by German painter, sculptor and graphic artist Georg Baselitz (b. 1938), shown at the British Museum exhibition *Germany Divided: Baselitz and his Generation* in 2014. It caused a furore in Dresden in 1962, but Baselitz was determined to change the saccharine complacency of postwar German art.

'She Speaks For Me' (p. 43):
   In 1990 in Los Angeles, Christa Wolf (1929-2011), East German writer and feminist, was lampooned for Stasi involvement. Eventually she remembered the one report she had written as a Party youngster, before her own thirty years under surveillance;
   The quotation in the 4th stanza comes from the East German poet Volker Braun in 'Property', *Rubble Flora* (p. 46), translated by David Constantine & Karen Leeder;
   The quotation in the fifth stanza is from Sigmund Freud.

'What the Angel Might Have Said in Response' (p. 46):
   Leuven University Library, Belgium, renowned for its mediaeval manuscripts, was destroyed by the German army in both August 1914 and May 1940. Its tower holds four large bells and a carillon of fifty-six.

'An African Carving' (p. 49):
   Cultivation began *c.*22,000 BCE, and dugouts date from 8,000 BCE;

one third of global food still comes from hoes and sickles; '...all to sweetness turns' is from Edward Thomas's poem 'Digging (I)';
The words 'When Adam delved and Eve span, who was then the gentleman?', come from an open-air sermon delivered in Blackheath by the preacher John Ball in 1381, shortly after the beginning of the Peasants Revolt.

'Devouring Time, Blunt Thou the Lion's Paw' (p. 51):
The title of William Shakespeare's Sonnet 19.

'Violets at Tourrettes-sur-Loup' (p. 53):
The epigraph is from *Les Contrerimes* (1921) by Paul-Jean Toulet (1867-1920) — *Stranger, my scent is sweet. Pick me without remorse: / violets bear the smile of death.*

'Summer Jet Black' (p. 59):
In the final stanza reference is made to Pierre Soulages (1919-2022), the French painter, printmaker, and sculptor who was known as 'the painter of black'. In 2014, the Musée Soulages, dedicated to the display of his works including those he referred to as his *Outrenoir* (beyond black), was opened in his hometown of Rodez.

'Air's So Much More Than Empty Space' (p. 61):
This poem refers to the stairwell ceiling by Tiepolo (1696–1726) in the Prince-Bishop's Palace at Würzburg, Southern Germany, called by Napoleon 'the nicest parsonage in Europe'.

'Tin Pan Alley' (p. 65):
Lauzes are rounded thick stone slates.

'Layered Life' (p. 67):
Gimmickry is a trick to attract attention, and in the Philippines a night out with a friend.

AUTHOR'S ACKNOWLEDGEMENTS

Written over the last six years since my first collection, these poems have been fine-tuned by Gregory Warren Wilson's close reading – as poet, violinist and glasswork artist. Our several sessions each year are wondrous fun and my thanks to him are legion, as they are to dear Tom Wengraf for his support and endless word-mongering. Warm thanks to two treasured and deep-thinking writing groups: Alida Gersie and Edward Schieffelin in London, and the Treignac Stanza group in France. I'd like to mention Andrew Cooper and Ali Ball (each sadly no more) and Scott Elder as lift-off, sky-stretching friends.

Eighteen of these poems have appeared in the following journals: *Abridged, Dawntreader, French Literary Review, Green Ink Press, Littoral* (6), *Scintilla, Southlight* (2), *The Galway Review* (4) and *The Topographers' Arms*.

The poems breathe indebtedness to special places, and to the people and forces responsible for them over centuries – chiefly my family farm on the River Severn in Gloucestershire, a wide-windowed Edwardian first-floor flat in Muswell Hill in London, and the steep valleys of the North Aveyron in France.

BIOGRAPHICAL NOTE

Prue Chamberlayne's self-published collection *Locks Rust* (2019) was warmly reviewed in *Poetry Salzburg Review* as "full of marvels... [and] complex meditations on political times and political places". Her chapbook *Beware the Truth that's Manacled* (erbacce-press, 2022) tackles the psychic underworld of racial experience. Its review in *London Grip* found its language "body brutish and darkly cruel in resonance... [with] great sensitivity to linking sounds, timbre and meaning". A pamphlet *Pendulum* is underway, exploring absence, memory, silence and outsiderism in a Ugandan / British relationship.

Poetry came after English school-teaching, lecturing and writing in comparative social policy and biographical interpretive research, and since 2007, a rural project in Uganda. It began with marvellous courses at the Poetry School with Tamar Yoseloff and Graham Fawcett, followed by an MA from the University of East Anglia in 2010 with George Szirtes and Lavinia Greenlaw.

Prue Chamberlayne won fourth prize in the 2025 Kent and Sussex Poetry Society Competition judged by Kit Fan.